7 Steps

to Raising

Amazing Children

HOW TO INFLUENCE YOUR CHILD

CHARLES SMITH

Fulton Books, Inc.
Meadville, PA

Published by Fulton Books 2020

ISBN 978-1-64654-778-4 (paperback)
ISBN 978-1-63710-218-3 (hardcover)
ISBN 978-1-64654-779-1 (digital)

Printed in the United States of America

I talk a lot about my children and my mother in this book, but the real hero and the person I proudly dedicate this book to is my wife of thirty-plus years, Gail Smith. Without you, honey, there would be no children and no book. You have taught me so much, and your love for me has been unwavering. I thank you for our four daughters and for the love and trust you have always shown me. There would be no me, as you know me, without you. I love you with all my heart.

CONTENTS

FOREWORD

This book is about the joy I experienced in raising my amazing children. Growing up, I knew I wanted to have a family of my own and be an influential part of their lives. I was what you would call a momma's boy from childhood all the way to adulthood.

Being a momma's boy, I spent a lot of time around my mother and got to know her very well. I watched how she would deal with each one of my siblings and me. I noticed that my mother handled each of us differently, but yet she treated us all the same. I found myself studying the way she raised us, and it has stuck with me after all these years.

I want to share with you some of the basic things I learned from watching my mother and how she took time with each of us individually. I learned a lot from her and have used her principles to raise some amazing children of my own. Of all the things she taught me, the most important thing was my need for a personal relationship with Jesus Christ, the ultimate teacher.

Somebody has to know you before they can raise you. My mother got to know each of her children, and she dealt with us according to that knowledge. And then she passed us on to Jesus, who knew us best to do the rest. And finally, at the age of twenty-three, I went into the insurance business for myself. It was amazing how much I learned about raising children from that business. The business taught me about leadership, influence, and relationships. So after forty years in the insurance business, thirty years as children's pastor, and being a forever momma's boy, I want to share with you 7 steps to raising amazing children. I know these steps will make a difference in your life and the lives of your children for generations to come.

INTRODUCTION

There is nothing more frustrating than having someplace to go, but you don't know how to get there. There is not a GPS for it, no Siri to give directions, or no other device that can help you get where you are going in your quest of directing and influencing your children for their present good and their future.

If you should miss the opportunity of teaching and guiding your children, your lack of commitment can affect generations to come. It's pretty important that you get to the nurturing place with your children. When raising our children, we are trying to get them to a place called success. We have been told that children are a gift from God and that we should treasure our gifts.

It is sad to say, but so many of our children are falling by the wayside. Many of them are dropping out of school, some are committing senseless crimes, and others are committing suicide. Who is to blame, and how can this be? What can we do as parents to stop the loss of our precious children?

In the house or the apartment we live in, the builder started with a foundation first, the same goes for the building where you work. When raising our children, we have to start with a good foundation in order to have success in our efforts. When our children are small, that is the best time for foundation building.

Each child is different, but they all need basic easy to follow principles for their lives. Just like my mother, she had basic teaching principles for all of us. Her methods were different according to the personality of each child, but her love for each of us remained the same. The foundation we set for our children is designed to give them a successful and profitable life.

When our children are young, they bring us so much joy. However, for some families, when their children grow older, they bring them so much pain. Mr. Duncan, at Duncan's Toy Store on *Home Alone 2*, said that children brought him a lot of joy, as they do to everyone who appreciates them. I agree with him 100 percent.

Not only should we appreciate our children, but also we should raise them so others can appreciate them. I know you, and I have this in common, we want our children to be their best. That is why I am sharing and providing these 7 steps to raising amazing children.

CHOOSE WHO INFLUENCES YOU

Whether you recognize it or not, someone is influencing you on a daily basis. Who has the most influence on your life? Is it your career? Is it your peers, your parents, or is it God? When we were children, we didn't have a choice of who influenced us. It was either our parents or whoever was responsible for raising us, along with the people to whom they exposed us. In other words, our environment was controlled by the people who were responsible for raising us.

Wow! This is important to remember. So at the beginning of our lives, we were influenced by the people who raised us, whether they were good or bad. They were in charge of preparing an environment that would influence and impact our lives for the rest of our lives.

Now that we are grown and have children, wouldn't you agree that it's important that we know who the people were who had influence over us while growing up? It is important to look at what we learned because we are now responsible for bringing up our children in a wholesome environment.

The things we learned along the way will definitely play a major part in how we nurture our own children. We are going to be influencing and impacting our children for the rest of their lives. As adults, we can choose our sphere of influence. We have the ability to come and go as we like; however, our children don't have that option.

I grew up very poor in Mississippi, and my parents impacted my life in a powerful way. Some things were good and some things not so good. I can recall like it was yesterday, how the ice cream truck would come down the street with the music playing. All the children would run to their houses to get money and then run to the truck to buy ice cream.

I would do the same thing, run in the house to get money for ice cream, but I could never run to the truck like the other children. I remember my mom always said, she didn't have any ice cream money. Don't tell anybody, but for a long time, I thought there was a special kind of money that said ice cream on it, because surely, Momma had money but just not ice cream money.

How did that impact my life as a parent? Well, I had a hard time saying no to my children when they asked for things. I heard "no" so much while growing up that I chose to say yes more than no to my children. Was that influenced by a situation in my early childhood? You bet it was. We are often being influenced by other people in our lives. The inability to give us the simple things we wanted dealt a crushing blow to our young spirits. Some people take it negatively, and others take it in a positive way to do better by their children. I am saying that we make choices and act out according to how we have been raised. That is part of our human nature.

A lot of people will have an influence on your life. You have to decide who or what will impact and benefit you the most. We have a tendency to listen to people, and without realizing it, we will remember it and often repeat what was said or duplicate what was done. We fail to think about who it may affect others than ourselves.

I remember reading somewhere that the two things that will impact and influence your life the most are the books you read and the people you meet. I make it a point to share that with my children often. It is so important to realize that what we hear, what we say, what we read, and who we choose to spend time with are molding us to be the people that we are and who we are going to become later on in life.

That being said, you have to make a conscious decision to be a leader and not a follower. You must decide that you are not going to allow just anybody or just anything to speak into your life—accepting the fact that we don't know everything and that we need other people in our lives, and we are going to use the advice of others to accomplish great things. We need the wisdom of God in our lives, so we discern what we should keep and what we must leave behind.

The Bible states in Proverb 3:5–6 (NKJV), "Trust in the Lord with all your heart, and lean not on your own understanding; in all your ways acknowledge Him, and He shall direct your paths."

An important step in raising amazing children for me was to make a conscious decision to trust in the Lord and not lean on my own limited understanding. I decided that I would acknowledge him and allow God's word and prayer to be the first and foremost influence in my life. Once you make the decision to trust God and allow him to influence your life, you will experience great power and security. When you realize that you are not alone to do all the things you need to accomplish, it's an amazing and relaxing feeling.

Raising children in this world can be scary and overwhelming! Dear parents, be calm when you take the first step in raising your amazing children. You are not alone in your endeavor. Choose God and allow him to lead you. I can remember calling on him so many times, and he was always there for me with resounding results.

I remember one particular time, my daughter Tara wanted to watch a movie at the house. Well, being mindful of the Lord and his presence, I had decided that I would not watch a movie at the house that was rated R. Neither would I allow a movie that was not suitable for the Smith children regardless of the rating.

Needless to say, the movie she wanted to watch was rated R, and according to her, everyone in the world had seen the movie except her and her siblings. She couldn't understand why I was so strict with them and wouldn't allow them to watch the movie. After all, she explained that she had heard all the curse words at school anyway. According to her, "It's just a movie." So what's the point in not watching, especially since everyone else in the world had watched it?

Parents, you have all heard it before. Our children want to do what is popular and wear what's in style. It's just the way of the world, and it is something that we have to deal with. But it is the way we deal with these things that will make or break us. So I stood my ground like I should have and said we shouldn't watch stuff that could affect us negatively.

In my opinion, there is a reason these movies have a rating and say you must be seventeen years old or older. But I tell you that did not go over well with her at all. She really wanted to watch that movie, and I have to say I love her determination. When she wanted something, she would not let it go easily.

I had given my children the right to say anything they wanted to say to me as long as it was done in a respectful way. This daughter would always push those limits. She would often ask me, "Daddy! Is this respectful?"

I would say, "Yes. Go ahead with your questions or concerns."

It was very important for me to keep the lines of communication open with my children at all costs. But obviously, if you have to ask if this is respectful before you ask the question, you are pushing it. With my final decision not going in her favor, she went on a rampage.

She started telling me she could not wait until she was eighteen years old. Tara listed all the things she was going to do when she reached that age. She was going to go to the casinos. She was going to go to the clubs and watch all the movies she wanted. I mean, she was some kind of mad. You could hear the tremble in her little voice. You would have thought that this movie was the best movie ever.

I listened very carefully to each word that was spoken without a clue as to how I would respond. I knew that my baby girl needed comforting. I stood there, clueless. It was not like me to respond and add to the anger that she was feeling. I could understand wanting something and not being able to have it.

As a parent, I needed to offer advice, not in a loud voice or a negative tone. I needed my message to be clear and comforting to her at the same time. I believe our spoken words and the way we deliver them to our children are forever influencing and impacting them. To me, this was a very important moment my daughter and I were having, and I needed more than my limited understanding to rely on.

At that moment, I heard Proverb 3:5–6, "Trust in the Lord with all your heart, and lean not on your own understanding; in all your ways acknowledge Him, and He will make your path straight."

I had learned this scripture. It was in my spirit, and I needed this for my baby girl. She was hurting, and it was because she didn't understand the rules. It wasn't because of the rule but a lack of understanding it.

Now it was my job to clarify the rule at that moment, so in a calm and relaxed voice, I spoke these words, "Sweetie, you can go anywhere you want to go, do anything you want to, and watch whatever movies you want to watch when you turn eighteen, as long as it is pleasing to the God you serve because he will be wherever you are and see whatever you are doing, not me."

I tell you, you would have thought God had shown up himself. There was complete silence on her part. You could have heard a pin drop as she walked back to her room. The words that followed from her mouth let me know that the words that I had just spoken were clear, understandable, impactful, and influential.

Her voice rang out from the back room, loud enough for me to hear her. They filled the kitchen where I was cooking. With these sweet words, she said, "Well, I might not do everything." I knew at that exact moment, the omnipresent God was right on time. He touched her heart.

Being influenced or led by the Lord is important to your success as a parent. It is the first step in raising amazing children. You see, this first step is the most important step. If you don't commit to following God, then you are in the dark about leadership as a parent. And without him, you are lost, blind, and confused about your own life. Without him, we can do nothing!

Please tell me how a lost, blind, and confused person can lead anyone anywhere that's going to be good for them? Go ahead. I am waiting!

Romans 9:1 (NKJV) says, "As long as I am in the world, I am the light of the word."

You see, unless we know which way to go, we will always be following someone else and will end up doing what they think is right.

But Jesus said, "I am the way, the truth, and the life. No one comes to the Father except through me" (John 14:6, NKJV).

So to be influenced by God, you have to accept his son Jesus Christ. I like to say, if you don't want to be left behind, he is the best choice.

Romans 10:9 says, "That if you confess with your mouth the Lord Jesus and believe in your heart that God has raised Him from the dead, you will be saved."

We have to be right to get it right for our children. We can't be wrong and get it right for them. I have a suggestion. It is the one I follow for my life. Make sure you get right with Jesus first and watch him work in your life. Chose Jesus and ask him to come into your life and save you.

We all need help to raise amazing children, and Jesus is the way. He helps us to be amazing as we trust in him. If we are going to be an example for our children, we need his guidance all the way. Our children watch our every move, and we cannot afford to blow our opportunity. We need to accept the life that God has for us that he has provided through his son Jesus Christ so we can let his light shine through us, and our children won't have to live in the dark.

Our children will realize that we are limited, but the God we serve is not. He is omnipresent, and he is our leader. In step one, we learned that we must build a personal relationship with Jesus Christ in order to lead our children right. We need him to guide us so we can raise amazing children.

I recall how God instructed me to think outside of the box and have fun and spend happy times with my children. I knew my children were special because they were a gift from God. My relationship with God was like no other. I felt like God and I had bonded, and I was his favorite person in this world. I needed to keep working on our relationship because it could be so much better.

I still had so much to learn and so much room to grow. So I just kept reading his word, praying to him, and writing songs to praise his name. I still feel that way about God and our relationship. We should all feel that way about our Creator because we are special to him. Jesus's death on the cross is all the evidence we need.

I heard the Lord speak to my heart and tell me to treat my children special like he treated me. Now before we go any further, let me explain. Regardless of how well I treat my children, it will never measure up to the great, marvelous, superior, awesome treatment that God provides for us every day. But I heard him say, "You are special to me. Treat them like they are special to you because they are a gift from me." I started to think of ways I could treat them special.

Once a week, we established a doughnut day. So every week, they had something to look forward to. It created excitement and established a bond with the girls. I could hear my girls talking the night before doughnut day, and one of them would say, "I am going to hurry up and get ready for bed because tomorrow is doughnut day." It was like going to bed would make the night go by faster.

If I was going to be late getting home because of a late appointment, I would stop by the house for lunch and bake some cookies for them. I would wrap them in aluminum foil in four different stacks and write their names on them with a marker: Tanya, Tara, Chara, and Amber. Just imagine walking into the house, looking on the counter, and seeing a treat with your name on it. You are going to feel pretty special.

My oldest daughter Zatanya, who we called Tan or Tanya, loved biscuits. Well, that's an understatement. This child really loved biscuits. I started to call her biscuit. Tan's school would start a little later than the younger children, and every morning, we would stop and get a biscuit and sometimes two for her—not a biscuit and bacon or biscuit and sausage but a plain biscuit. But for the price of a biscuit, sometimes two, and the conversations we had were priceless, and the memories will live on forever.

When you connect with God, you find ways to connect with his gifts, which are your precious children, he blessed you with. Later, I started taking each of my children out for dinner on their birthday. We dressed up like we were ready for church and went to a nice place for dinner. Our favorite place was the University Club. It was on the twenty-first or twenty-third floor, and we would always sit by a window so we could look down on the city and up at the stars while we enjoyed an elegant meal. There was confetti on the table with balloons and a sign that read happy birthday, while the pianist played and sang happy birthday to my child.

When they got a little older, I allowed them to bring a friend along. That made it even more special to watch them communicate with their friends and to know what kind of friends they were keeping company with and, most of all, to show them how special they are to their father and how they are to be treated by other men. And as my heavenly Father so lovingly cares for me, I want to reciprocate (give back) that special love to my amazing children. I understand that it was God's love for me that taught me how to show love as well.

My baby Amber and I used to go to the University Club for breakfast every Friday. It was a special time, and she would always get one of those big cinnamon rolls. The cinnamon roll was as big as she was. She would get the cinnamon roll after she had eaten grits, eggs, bacon, sausage, and orange juice. She was skinny, but that little Amber could really eat. I would just watch her as she enjoyed herself with her dad. We would just sit there and talk about everything.

This one particular Friday morning, she was talking about how the children would always ask her about a place to go out and eat because they thought she had gone to all the nice places in Jackson, Mississippi, with her mom and dad. You could tell she was proud to be the one that her classmates would ask where the nice places to dine for dinner were.

She told me if she was a few minutes late, her classmates would ask her, "Where have you been this morning, Amber?" And before she could answer, they would say, "At the University Club for breakfast, I bet." She would always answer with excitement and say yes.

She was very happy about the time we were spending together. Listening to her stories of her classmates made me proud too. Then she told me something that made me delighted that I knew Jesus. She said, "Dad, thank you for taking the time to bring me up here for breakfast on Fridays. I know you have to go to work, but you always bring me, and I thank you."

Okay, give me a second to wipe away the tears from my eyes! Even now, it affects me emotionally when I think about my little daughter expressing so much gratitude for a simple act as a weekly breakfast. I am so glad that I know God, and he instructed me to show love to my children. I fought back the tears and said, "You are welcome, sweetie. I wouldn't miss it for the world."

You may be thinking, well, I am late getting started. No problem. God is excited that you are ready now, and he will guide you the rest of the way. He is never too busy for you. And your child will be glad to see Christ in you.

My baby Chara was in a play in elementary school, and it was her first play ever. It was easy to see that she was a natural at acting. I could see why the teachers had her playing the main character. She was dressed as a little old lady with a silver wig on her head. She wore a long brown dress with a big white collar. She was excellent! Her mother and I were so proud. You could tell her acting ability came from her mother. My wife Gail is a tremendous actress and loves to participate in our church plays.

We were sitting in the audience on the second or third row, and Chara didn't see us right off. We were both admiring her performance. Then all of a sudden, you could tell she spotted us, and she waved her hand excitedly. In the middle of her performance, at that second, we were the only ones in that auditorium that mattered to her. Then she gathered herself and performed even better than before. I didn't know she was going to stop and wave like that, but you better believe we were all smiles.

Regardless of where you have been or what you have done, once you acknowledge Christ in your life like he is the only one that matters, your child will reciprocate that same love.

Things to Remember

1. All of us have been influenced by someone.
2. We make choices and behave according to how we were raised.
3. We are responsible for raising our children in a wholesome environment.
4. If a parent wants their children to follow them, they must be consistent leaders.
5. It is important to have clear and constant rules for your family.
6. Keep the lines of communication open with your children.
7. Parents are the key influencers in their children's lives.
8. The best wisdom for raising children comes from God through prayer and study of his word.
9. When saying no to your children, be tactful.
10. Establish a special time to get together with your children. Make it a practice to spend time with them.

Reflections

1. What do I need to let go of from my past that would hinder me from raising amazing children?

_____

_____

_____

_____

_____

2. What three rules will I put in place to better myself as a parent?

_____

_____

_____

_____

_____

My Prayer

_____

_____

_____

_____

_____

_____

_____

_____

_____

_____

STEP 2

ENCOURAGE YOUR CHILDREN TO READ THE BIBLE

Now that we know the source of our influence or our strength, it is time for us to start encouraging our children. Let's start with the Word of God.

Proverbs 5:7 (KJV) reads, "Therefore, hear me now, my children, and do not depart from the words from my mouth."

When you read Bible stories to your children, you are teaching them the Word of God, and you are influencing them to read the Word of God for themselves. If you want to raise amazing children, start with the Word of God. When your children see you reading the Bible and you are reading the Bible to them as well, this is huge in their eyesight.

Before they go to bed each night, they should know that a Bible story will be read to them by you. Let me ask you, "How powerful do you think this is in the eyes of your children?" Let me tell you, this will be some of the most important and powerful times you will ever spend with your children, as you talk about the most important person in their life, their Creator.

I know you thought I was going to say you. You are important because you are the one who is introducing them to our Creator. So for now, you are the most important person in their little eyes. Each time you read to them, you are presenting something that will go with them all their lives. Every night will be special for them as they learn even more important things about God and his wonderful love for them.

As you read God's Word to your children, you are building a bridge. You are creating a bridge where your children can cross over and connect with their omnipotent and omnipresent God. Your role as mentor and nourisher will cause them to see things differently through their eyes of faith. So your job is to bridge them over so they can be permanently connected. Wow! How important is that connection?

Think with me for a minute. Can you see how easy it is for many people to miss out on this simple but important process? Once you make the connection with the Savior yourself, you start thinking, *How can I help my children connect as well?* This will become so important to you because most of us want better for our children than we had for ourselves.

Our children are a gift from God to us. We are responsible for teaching and training them so that they will choose him. That is how we give them back to God. We can't raise them on our own. We need the Lord's help! Let that sink in for a minute. We are only here on earth for a short period of time, and we can't save anybody, but we can point them to the Savior.

It should be our goal to be the best bridge we can be for our children. Webster has a definition of bridge that reads, "Something that is intended to reconcile or form a connection between two things." In this case, your children and the Almighty God.

The Bible says that Christ reconciled us to God in II Corinthians 5:20 (NKJV), "Now then, we are ambassadors for Christ, as though God were pleading through us: we implore you on Christ's behalf, be reconciled to God."

You are the main influence, not the church, not the pastor or any other ministry, but you are the main bridge that will lead your children. Not that it doesn't take a village to help raise a child, but let's face it, you are the first and the main bridge. That's how you should want it. You are not second fiddle to anyone when it comes to introducing Christ to your children through the Bible. Your prayers and the time you spend reading and teaching them make the connection successful. So take it seriously. It's a permanent connection you are making between your child and their Savior.

I remember once, my children were waiting on me to come and read them their Bible story. I guess I was taking too long for them, and Amber, our baby, came to the kitchen where I was and asked, "Daddy, are you going to read our Bible story tonight?" Man, you should have seen me running to that room to read that Bible story to them.

Did you notice how she said it? She said, "Are you going to read 'our' Bible story?" That's taking ownership early in life, wouldn't you say. That's allowing the Word of God to take over for you as you build that bridge. You know this is such an important step because once you get the Word in your children, it stays there and will not come back void.

Isaiah 55:11 (NKJV) says, "So shall My word be that goes forth from My mouth; It shall not return to Me void, but it shall accomplish what I please, and it shall prosper in the thing for which, I sent it." Let me explain that as you are reading to your children each night, an exchange is taking place. That word is getting and remaining in their hearts. The scripture says, "God's word won't come back void, and it will accomplish what I please." All I can say is *wow*!

You see, you can't go wrong with reading and teaching your children the Word of God. It is your children's shield of protection. And listen, it also says, "And it shall prosper in the thing for which I sent it." You are setting your child up for greatness by introducing the Word of God to them right now. Their eyes, ears, and hearts are open wide to receive the Lord as their Savior.

God is pleased with us when we feed our children spiritual food. He is also pleased that we are receiving life from the Word that we pass on to them. What I am about to tell you next is going to bless your mind. I need you to be sitting down. While you are sitting, will you go ahead and get a pad, a pen, or a highlighter as well. I don't want you to miss this. You will want to write this down.

Listen, not only are you passing the Word of God on through your children but also this is generational. Yes, you are leaving a legacy, not just for your children but your grandchildren, great-grandchildren, and your great-great-grandchildren. And it all started with you.

I asked Siri to give me a definition of legacy, and here is what she had to say, "An amount of money or property left to someone in a will." It also said, "A thing handed down by a predecessor." Webster had a similar definition. I am here to tell you that it's good if you can leave money. It's great if you have a property to pass on. But whether or not you have money or property, you can connect them to Jesus now, and you don't have to leave him in a will, and your offspring will have him to pass on for generations to come.

Now compare Jesus with any amount of money or property, and I guarantee you that Jesus will come up a winner every time. I have a recommendation for you. Seek first the kingdom of God for your children, and I know how they will turn out. Another way I introduced the Word of God to my children was through music. I would take a scripture from the Bible and create a song with a beat to it like a jingle and sing it to my children.

They still remember the songs today. Listen, music is a universal language, and if you have some rhythm to it, they will never forget it. Children really enjoy songs. I hear you saying, "But I can't sing." Welcome to my world. When I sing, adults dial 911 because they think that I am being attacked. That's why I love working with children. They just go with the flow and say, "Sing it again." Trust me, they will think it's cute, and you will be having such an impact on their lives, and they don't even know it.

Our job is to get them in the Word as soon as possible and as often as possible. So let's have some fun and help make life better for them. It's your duty and responsibility to influence them to follow you as you follow Christ.

Things to Remember

1. You are the most important person in your child's eyes.
2. You are the bridge that leads them to Christ.
3. Set a standard in your home with the Word of God.
4. Be consistent in reading the Bible to your children.
5. Children learn what is really important by your example.
6. It takes time to train your children in the right principles.
7. The Word of God is your child's shield of protection.
8. Music helps to enhance what you teach your children.
9. How you nurture your children greatly influences their future.
10. What you teach your children will impact your family for generations to come.

Reflections

1. How dedicated am I to my children's Bible knowledge?

_____

_____

_____

_____

_____

2. Here are the steps I will take to spend time with my children in Bible reading:

   - Set a time for Bible reading.
   - Commit to being consistent.
   - Make it a priority regardless of other things.
   - Do it with joy.

3. I promise I will draw closer to God so that my children will have a parent who genuinely loves the Lord.

4.   My prayer to God

_____

_____

_____

_____

_____

_____

_____

SHOW YOUR CHILDREN HOW TO PRAY

I wrote a poem in memory of my mother.

My Mom

My mom and I, together, we'll always be,
My mom truly loved me, and I loved her,
We shared that love until the day she died,
To be with the man who carried her while she
carried me.
For nine months, she carried me,
For twenty-eight years, she was a guide for me.
We shared that love until the day she died,
To be with the man who carried her while she
carried me.
My mom was ready for this day, that I know,
And she asked me to be ready also.

So you see, my mom and I will be together again because I will
be ready just like her.

I wrote this poem to be placed in my mother's obituary when she died in 1985. My mother was a great example to me as to how to raise children. I have often said that if I could be half the parent that my mother was, then I would be a great parent. Yes, I said half the parent because my mother was just that amazing.

What she taught me was wonderful. By just watching her deal with us was mesmerizing. One of the biggest lessons I learned was what was needed to raise a child. I grew up with three brothers and three sisters. I had four brothers, but one drowned at a young age. I remember that incident like it was yesterday. My mother had to go down to the funeral home and identify his body. I was the baby at the time, and I could not have been more than four or five years old when she viewed his body. The only thing my precious mother could say while crying uncontrollably was "That's my son. That's my son!"

Growing up with my siblings, I remember my mother praying for us while on her knees, calling each of us by name, asking the Lord to protect and guide us. She had a thing for praying out loud. I must say that was a very important thing because I learned from her to always pray. I suppose the tragic death of her oldest child inspired her to always pray for us.

She would spend the same amount of time praying for all her children. I often thought that she should spend more time on my siblings and less time praying for me because I was the good child, so I thought. I actually told her, "Sonny and Mane [these were my brothers' nicknames] need more prayer time than I do."

I was the good child, and they stayed in trouble. I never gave her any trouble at all. It seems to me that she started to pray for me even longer after I made that statement. I guess Mom knew that it wasn't about what we did or didn't do because our good deeds couldn't save us. She was an amazing lady. She knew prayer worked, and I didn't know anything and was just running my mouth.

Watching my mother pray was an important lesson in how to raise children. My father was not around, so it was just Mom. She was left on her own to raise the seven of us. That's what I thought, but Mom had a different view than I did when it came to raising children. I would later learn that it was not about her, and she knew it. Mom placed all her trust in the Lord, and she believed that with God, all things were possible, and she lived her life accordingly.

Her attitude was always positive, and she never stopped encouraging her children to believe that we could do anything that we wanted to, if we would just pray to God and trust in him. And what I am sharing with you in this book is what I learned from an amazing lady who I called Mom.

Again, one of the first lessons I learned was to pray. Prayer is powerful, and the power of prayer needs to be understood. How do you influence your children to pray? You may be thinking that's crazy! Children should pray because there is a God, and that's how we communicate with him.

We pray because we should. First of all, let's look at influence. What does it mean? *Influence is the capacity to have an effect on the character, development, or behavior of someone or something or the effect itself (to have someone follow you).*

Who are you? You are the parents who are raising amazing children—whether you had them yourself, adopted them, or maybe they are just in your house, and you are responsible for raising them. You are the influencer, and you need to know that "things just don't happen. Someone has to make them happen."

My pastor, Bishop Ronnie Crudup Sr., makes that statement all the time. So we don't get caught up on what's supposed to happen, but we focus on what we want to happen when it comes to raising our children, and prayer works!

As parents, you get the first chance to influence your children for their good. Your children will have to deal with temptations for the rest of their lives, and what you encourage them to do while they are young will be with them forever. Think about that statement. "Forever" is never-ending. That makes our godly influence one of the key elements in raising amazing children.

Here is why your godly influence over your children is so important. While they are small, they are looking at you as their god. Yes, I said it. You are their god while they are small, and they look or depend on you for everything. Yes, everything—food, clothing, shelter, and guidance. You should be the first to introduce your child to the god you serve and to the god you pray to.

The belief that you are god is short-lived, and when I say short-lived, I mean, short-lived. That's why you have to capture the time to influence them while the window of opportunity is open. The power to influence or guide will shift as your children get older. Their teachers, friends, peers, and pastor, along with a lot of other people, will have their attention.

Here are some things that worked for me, and I believe they will work for you as well. After you finish reading Bible stories with your children, then pray with them, but before you start, you ask them if they have anyone that they want you to pray for.

If they are in kindergarten or early elementary, you are opening yourself up for a long prayer, but it's important that you do it. They are going to name all their friends. Our baby Amber was the talkative one, and she would want to pray for everyone in her class. She knew how to get our attention.

I can remember when she was about two years old going on three. We were all standing around her bed, talking a lot, and all my girls wanted to get their story in, so I would hear what they had to say. Because she was the smaller one, often, her voice would be drowned out by the older girls. They had my attention more than she did.

Well, this particular night, we were standing around, conversing, and like always, she was being talked over. Her sisters were saying, "Daddy, Daddy, Daddy!" Then all of a sudden, I heard my baby girl in her soft voice say, "My daddy!" I don't know where she got that from, but it got my attention immediately, and I quickly acknowledged her. It is amazing what you start with your children when they are young. Now that they are older, we still gather around each other and just talk for hours. You won't always feel like praying for what seems like everybody at the school, but you can't shortcut this process. It's too important to your child's early prayer life-learning experience. Even today, I am still praying for friends of my girls.

What a blessing it is for your children to be influenced by you to pray. It can last forever. You are showing them early in life the importance of being in God's presence. They are learning that you are serving a mighty God who answers prayer. It is important that they know early in life that you know who is ultimately in charge of this world and that Jesus is the one who we are praying to every night.

Kneeling down in prayer with your children is a beautiful memory for them to have of you. I believe that our God smiles every time he sees his children pray and read his word. Now imagine the everlasting image you are passing on to your children.

I wrote a song about praying and taught it to my own children and the children that were in the children's church. I taught it to the entire church. It became a popular song at New Horizon Church International, where I attend. The song is entitled "When I Pray, It's No Time to Play."

I realize that music is a universal language, and it's a great tool in teaching your children, whether you are teaching them to pray or learning scripture. Let me say that you don't have to write a song or come up with music in order to teach your children to pray. Neither is it necessary to use the method we have here at our church. There are plenty of songs out there that you can use.

I am also going to make the songs that I have written available to you as well. I shared with you earlier that we are not perfect. Now I am telling you, we don't know everything or have everything that it takes to raise amazing children, but we do have to use the resources that are available to us.

When I first started writing songs, I felt that I should be the one to sing them. Okay! You don't know me, and you haven't heard me sing. If you have heard me sing, you know that God did not give me the gift of singing. Don't worry about your voice. If singing helps you to deliver a special message to your children, then, by all means, sing! I got that revelation one day that I should let the children sing the songs that I write. Wow! What a thought that was. It has been so amazing ever since then.

To hear the children sing about loving Jesus and praying to Jesus will bring tears to your eyes every time. Prayer is communicating with God, and we must guide our children in their prayers.

However, when you do it, you have to be intentional and consistent while teaching them to pray.

Once your children fall in love with praying, they are going to want to pray about everything. That's perfectly okay, and you don't want to discourage it. We would rather have them wanting to pray about everything with excitement than them not wanting to pray at all.

Remember, you can't influence your child to pray if you are not praying. Luke 18:1 (NKJV) says, "Then He spoke a parable to them that men always ought to pray and not lose heart."

I have always tried to do the right thing by my children. I am aware that each one of them is different and has their own temperament. It is so important to remember what they do should not determine how they are treated. My time spent in God's presence will be the deciding factor on how I treat my children.

Dear parent, the more time you spend with God in prayer will determine how well prepared you will be for the challenges that you are going to face with your children. And yes, you are going to face some challenges. So the question is "Are you willing to spend the time in prayer to be more prepared for the challenges that are guaranteed to come?"

The more you pray, the better you are able to influence your child to pray. It becomes your DNA. And even after doing all that, you are still human, and you will make mistakes.

One of my biggest mistakes in my eyes was when one of my twins, Chara, did something that deserved punishment. Now I never just punished my children without listening to them explain what happened. Even if it was obvious, a punishment was justified. It's called respecting the child. My sweet little girl Chara gave me all her reasons why she did what she did.

She expressed how sorry she was. She had *prayed* for forgiveness and said it wouldn't happen again. Well, either she is a great negotiator, or I am a sucker. Either way, I decided not to punish her. Besides, I very seldom had to get on her about anything. All children deserve a little latitude.

After all, the child asked God to forgive her. Well, that would have been okay if I had left it at that and said, "Okay, you are forgiven. Go and sin no more," like Jesus did, right? But I am not Jesus. I can sometimes get in the flesh and do exactly what he says not to do.

God said in Colossians 3:21 (NKJV), "Fathers, do not provoke your children, lest they become discouraged." I am almost ashamed to tell you what happened next. It was so out of character for me. But because it showed me how much more I needed to pray and lean on God, I am sharing this with you. It is important that we watch and pray then pray some more.

I looked at my daughter, and I said, "Chara, I am not going to punish you because you haven't given me much trouble at all. Now don't you ever do that again. Do you understand?"

Chara said, "Yes, sir!"

I said, "If you were your sister Tara, girl, you would be on punishment for the rest of your life!" Do you understand me?

With a slight grin on her face, she said, "Yes, sir!"

"Now you can go back to your room," I said.

I was talking to Chara in her big sister's room for privacy because I didn't want the other children to hear or see me disciplining one of their siblings. It is called respecting the child. But I knew immediately that I had done wrong to one child by trying to do right by the other.

Did I just do that? God, please forgive me. OMG! I literally could not move, so I just sat there praying. I needed to feel the presence of God forgiving me, and I knew that's not what I should have been searching for because Jesus died for our sins, past, present, and future. But I just wanted to feel something. I needed comforting.

But what I heard was confrontation coming. All I could hear were giant footsteps coming up the hallway. Here is how the conversation went when Chara made it back to the room.

Tara asked, "Did Dad punish you for what you did?"

Chara replied, "No, he let me slide this time and told me not to do it again."

Tara said, "He let you slide!"

Chara said, "Yea! But he said that if I were you, he would punish me for life."

So the giant footsteps I heard coming up the hall was from a nine-year-old calling my name. "Daddy!" She knocked on the door and came in. Tara continued, "Daddy! I know you didn't punish Chara for what she did, but did you tell her that if she were me, you would have punished her for life because I always get in trouble, and she doesn't ever get in trouble?"

I said, "Lord, where are you? Now, Tara, I didn't quite say it like that, but what I did say was wrong, and I am sorry. I always look for the good you guys do, and I have let you slide without punishing you when you have done something wrong, haven't I?"

Tara replied, "Yes, sir."

"But your name should never come up when I am disciplining one of your siblings. I am sorry!"

And boy, I tell you, I was truly sorry. Why would a parent provoke their child like that? I prayed with a broken heart and asked the Lord to help me guide my children. I owned up to my mistake, and I felt the presence of his forgiveness. I was instructed to talk about forgiveness during our Bible story time, and afterward, we prayed for God to forgive us of our sins. My broken heart was mended. To inspire your children to pray, teach them I Thessalonians 5:17 (NKJV) that said, "Pray without ceasing!"

Things to Remember

1. Continual prayer is necessary in raising children.
2. Prayer gives you the strength to deal with every challenge.
3. Prayer is communicating with God. Talk to him first each day.
4. Whatever your relationship is with the children in your care, it takes prayer to raise them.
5. As parents, we get the first chance to influence our children for their good.
6. There is only a small window of opportunity to nurture your children. Don't miss it!
7. Even though we pray, we can miss the mark, but don't stop praying.
8. Our power to influence our children changes as they get older.
9. Teaching children to pray is important in building their relationship with Jesus Christ.
10. Living a life of prayer helps us to forgive ourselves and others.

Reflections

1. What I remember most and cherish about a loved one praying.

_____

_____

_____

_____

2. I will be an example for my children as a praying parent. Therefore, I will do the following:

    •   Set a specific time and place for prayer.
    •   Let them hear me pray.

- Encourage them to pray and include others.
- Pray and read scriptures with them.
- Tell them we are talking directly to God.
- Teach them that God answers our prayers.
- Keep a prayer journal.

3. My personal prayer commitment

_____

_____

_____

_____

_____

BE ACTIVE IN CHURCH WITH YOUR CHILDREN

Having a place of worship for your family is vital to you being able to influence your children with godly principles. Your church is like a second home, where you go to be fed the Word of God and to be energized for the week to come. When choosing a church home, do your research and make sure that the one you pick has a place that will attend to your children's spiritual needs.

As sure as they need food for their physical body to grow and be healthy, they also need spiritual food to grow spiritually fit. As parents, we are directly responsible that all those needs are met. At my home church, New Horizon Church International, in Jackson, Mississippi, we have children's ministry, youth ministry, and young adult ministry. These ministries were effective when our girls were growing up and are still effective today. You have heard that it takes a village to raise a child, and your home church is that village.

We have children's church for ages five to eleven years old for services on Sunday and on Wednesday night, and nursery for ages four and under. We have a bridge class for ages twelve and thirteen years old, who may not be quite ready for the youth at this point in their lives. The youth ministry ages are fourteen to nineteen, and we have a young adult ministry starting at age twenty. We also have a

children choir, youth choir, young adult choir, children dance ministry, youth dance ministry, young adult dance ministry, and we have a
mime ministry for our young people as well. Plus, we have an annual
children's revival that is designed just for the children. We also have
a huge Holy-ween celebration on October 31 each year as an alter-
native to Halloween.

By now, you get the point. Your home church may or may not
have all these ministries, but the idea is that your children are going
to a place where they can enjoy and learn at the same time. When I
say you have to influence your children to attend church, you have
to make sure that the church is catering to your child first of all, and
that's on you. With the right settings in place at your church, you can
start to influence your precious children.

How can we influence our children to attend church? First, let
me say this. Our children need to be taken to church and not sent
to the church. I hear you saying, "Well, as long as I get them there,
that should be the only thing that matters." No! No! No! It's greater
than that! We cannot influence them to do right if we are not fully
committed.

We have to get them involved in church and be involved to
influence them to be excited. There is no excuse for a parent and
child not to be active in their church. Our children need to feel like
they belong to and own a part of the church. Here is what I meant
when I said belong and own. Take an active part in something at the
church.

Show your children the importance of belonging by taking part
in some part of the ministry that is designed for you. It is our example that does the influencing! We are talking about taking our children to church and being an example to them. We send our children
to school to learn to read and write. We take our children to church
to learn which way is right. Your presence there makes a world of
difference. They will feel connected.

You are the leader doing the right thing by leading them to
Christ with their church attendance. That is what influence is all
about—getting your child to follow you while you follow Christ.
When they become involved in the ministry activities of the church,

they will feel like they belong to the ministry and are a part of that organization. How awesome is that for a child to feel connected to something that is about worshipping our Lord and Savior Jesus Christ.

Wow! Now your child is excited and asking you to take them to practice, and they are singing the songs and doing the dance routines in the dance ministry. They want you to see what they have learned. How impactful is that, my friends!

Can you see the difference? You are not just sending them to church, and all they think about is getting out of the church and going home. No! Now they are excited about what is taking place in their lives. You brought them to church and got them involved, and now they can't wait to come to church. Having your child involved in church activities and watching them participate in the church is a beautiful thing to watch.

Now that our children are involved, we must do the next best thing. I hear you asking, "What is it?" I am glad you asked. It's now your turn to get involved if you are not already! That's right. You need to be involved as well. You may say, "I can't sing," "I can't dance," "I don't have that kind of talent," and "I don't have time."

The Bible says in Matthew 9:37 (NKJV), "The harvest truly is plentiful, and the laborers are few."

If you can't sing, dance, mime, or act, you can volunteer to help out in children's church, help with the youth, help in the nursery, be a greeter, be an usher, help with the parking, help out in the kitchen, help out somewhere.

Your child needs to know that you are involved, and they need to see you involved. We all have heard the old adage "Do as I say and not as I do." Forget that you ever heard that. It doesn't apply to you. You are trying to influence your children for good. Children need a role model to follow, and who could be better than their parents. You don't have to do the same thing all the time. You may feel a need to change activities or ministries until you find your real calling.

If your child is involved in church activities and you are not, that is a hindrance to God's plan for your child's life. As beautiful as it is for you to see your child singing in the choir or dancing on the dance team, it is just as powerful for them to see you working within a ministry at the church. My friend, this is called winning. You have a purpose and a plan for your child's life, and God has a bigger plan.

The Lord placed parents in charge of leading and guiding their children. He wants to direct their steps and bless their lives to prosper. With his help, we work fervently as good parents, grandparents, guardians, ministers, or pastors over our children.

I remember one Saturday, I was out in my home office working on a project for my business. I was deeply involved and didn't want to stop. I could hear the outside door open to the house, but you had to come through another door to get to my office. And that door was closed.

So I knew a child was coming, but I couldn't tell who it was. The rule was that even if my car is in the garage but my office door is closed, it's just like I am not home, so allow Daddy to work and don't disturb him. That rule never did work. Now I heard a knock on the door, and she yelled, "Daddy!"

"Yes, who is it?" I asked.

"It's Tara!"

Like I didn't know her voice. I just wanted verification of who is bending the rules.

"I need to go to church for dance practice," she said.

"Where is your mother?" I asked.

"Momma is on the phone and said she's going to take me when she gets off, but I can't be late, Daddy! Mrs. Kim wants us there on time, and I need to leave now. We are learning a new dance. Can you take me, please?"

This was before we had cell phones, so you couldn't drive and talk like you can now.

The first thought I had was that this girl never gets this excited about being on time for school. But today, she was asking me to stop what I was doing to take her to church for dance practice. The second thought I had was "Man, this is a blessing."

"Okay, let's go!"

Her mother would have gotten her there on time. She always did, but my child was just exploring her options because Daddy was home. What a blessing for my child to want to go to church even on a Saturday.

My children grew up watching my wife and I work in the children's ministry and later become the head of the children's ministry. I remember thinking that I may need to slow down at the church myself because I was getting burned out. My three older daughters had Mr. Henry Murphy as their youth pastor, and my baby had Ms. Marsha Traylor as her youth pastor. They would always come home and tell me about something that they had learned from their youth pastor. Honestly, I would always be excited about what they were learning.

There were times they would mention something that Mr. Murphy or Ms. Marsha said, and I would think to myself, *Now that's the same thing that I have been saying forever. They say it one time, and now they act like it's the golden rule.* So I thought, *How can I make what I say stick?* So I set up some time to talk to Mr. Murphy, the youth pastor.

I told him that I was hearing my daughters talking about what was said in the youth church, and it was amazing. I loved what it was doing for the girls, and I wanted it to continue to impact them even more. I will never forget what he said to me that blessed my life. He said, "Charles, you don't need to do anything more than you are already doing for them. You are doing an awesome job."

He continued to say that sometimes, our children just need to hear what you have said from someone else. Our job is to have them in the right place under the right leadership so they can hear what they need to hear as many times as they need to hear it. Then he told me how he appreciated what I was doing with the children's ministry. He said his son, Little Henry, came to him and said, "That song that Mr. Smith taught us in class. I cannot get it out of my head." This was exciting for me.

He was helping to instill the Word of God in my children in the youth ministry, and I was helping to instill the Word of God in his children in our children's ministry. That was so exciting for me to see how we tag-teamed to help our own children and the rest of the children of the church. *I can't slow down now. I need to kick it up a notch,*

I thought to myself. I thank you for that, Henry. Henry has gone on to be with the Lord now, but I will forever appreciate his words!

Thank God we are not alone in our efforts. "God said, 'I will never leave you nor forsake you'" (Hebrews 13:5, NKJV). Listen, I know you want to be your best in raising amazing children. So I am thankful that you are reading this book. I am excited for you because I know great things will take place in your child's life. I also want you to know that the church is just a beginning. Wherever your children are involved, you too should be involved, whether it's in their school, Boy Scouts, Girl Scouts, sports, and any other activities they participate in. Don't just send them there. Go with them. It will make a world of difference in their lives for the rest of their lives, and they will repeat it with their own children.

Things to Remember

1. Having a regular place of worship is vital to the spiritual growth of the family.
2. Don't just send your children to church—attend with them.
3. Let your children see you as an active member of the church.
4. Your involvement in the church will help your children feel like they belong.
5. Your child's knowledge about spiritual things will be enhanced by regular church attendance.
6. Encourage your child to take part in church activities.
7. Be excited about their involvement in the church.
8. Your children will learn to follow you as you follow Christ.
9. Your faithfulness in the church is your best example.
10. Your children learn what the Savior is like by attending church.

Reflections

1. Life is sometimes hectic, but I will lead my children to Christ and get them involved in church. My prayer to the Lord:

_____

_____

_____

_____

_____

_____

2. Church should be a place where my children can do the following:

- Grow spiritually.
- Meet people who can mentor them.
- Make friends.
- Be in activities suitable for their age.
- Have fun while they learn.
- Learn good habits.
- Feel they belong.
- Learn respect for other adults.
- Learn the importance of giving.

TEACH YOUR CHILDREN TO RESPECT YOU

We have all heard a mother, teacher, grandmother, or some other leader when questioned why we should follow their instructions say, "Because I said so." In other words, don't ask for an explanation. Just do what I said, and do it now. I have a question for you, "Do you respect that when you hear it?" Of course not! We all want to feel like our opinion matters, even when it doesn't. There are two things that will help you in teaching your children to respect you. They are the following:

1. Your words
2. Your actions

Let's look at your words. We have all heard the old saying "That sticks and stones may break my bones, but words will never hurt me." We know for a fact that is not true. Forget that you ever heard that! It is one of the biggest untrue statements that have ever been told. With your words, you are either pushing your child away from you or pulling them toward you.

When you converse with your child, your words need to be encouraging and uplifting. Even if the child is in trouble, you should always make sure you express to him or her that it's not them that you are upset with but their behavior.

We don't have bad children. We have children who do bad things. Through the use of the right words, you can show your child the importance of changing negative behavior and how to choose positive behavior. But if you are not careful with your words, you can push them so far away from you that they won't be able to hear you. There is no respect earned when they are so far from you. Keep them close to you with the right words in order to gain respect from them.

The best way to guard your words and be positive with your children is to stay in God's Word and draw closer to him. When you read and study your Bible and pray for the Lord's guidance in dealing with your children, your outcome will be successful. When you humble yourself before the Lord in prayer and ask him to have mercy on you and grant you the know-how in dealing with your children with humility, he will do it!

Let's look at Webster's definition of what the word humble means. First, because I know what many parents say concerning their children, let's deal with that first. I can hear you mumbling under your breath about you don't have to humble yourself to a child. "I brought them in this world, and I will take them out."

Here is what Webster has to say about humble—*not proud or haughty, not arrogant or assertive.*

Okay, Webster, what does haughty mean? Haughty means *blatantly and disdainfully proud, having or showing an attitude or superiority and contempt for people or things perceived to be inferior.*

Wow! Attitude or superiority—how many of us use these two adjectives when we are speaking to our children? I know, right! Let me encourage you to stop it!

In the book of Proverb 10:11, it states, "The mouth of the righteous is a well of life, but violence covers the mouth of the wicked" (NKJV), and Matthew 15:11 says, "Not what goes into the mouth defiles a man; but what comes out of the mouth, this defiles a man" (NKJV).

We are honoring God when we are humble and show respect to our children. When we approach issues with prayer and get the mind of God on how to precede that pleases him and lets our children know that this is how we deal with issues. Then our children will respect what we say and what we do.

God knows us best, but our children know us better than anyone else in the world. If the world wants to know us as parents, they should ask our children. When our children respect who we are, whom we belong to, and what we represent, they will gladly tell the world. If you want to have your children's respect as their parent, you have to carry yourself with respect, and they will learn from your example and duplicate it to the world.

Many of us just expect our children to respect us because we are the parents. It does not work like that. Respect is taught. It is not automatic. You have to earn it.

In the Bible, we find the answer to the question about how to get respect. The Bible teaches us in Proverbs 22:6 (NKJV), "Train up a child in the way he should go, and when he is old, he will not depart from it."

If you are training a horse, I have been told that you have to respect that horse. If you are training a lion or a tiger for the circus or any animal, you have to respect them, or you can be attacked. Now don't get me wrong. I am not calling our precious children animals, but hear me out here. If you train up a child in the way he or she should go when they are old, they will not depart from it either.

How can a person respect, have patience, and train their animals and not show that same patience, respect, and care in the training of their children? Okay, let me cut to the chase and get right to the point that I want to make. If you want your children's respect, you must show them love, joy, peace, long-suffering, gentleness, goodness, and faith. These are the fruit of the spirit from Galatians 5:22. When you show and demonstrate these, you can expect to be respected. Respect is not a one-way street. When you give it, you will receive it.

The Bible in Luke 12:48 (NKJV) says, "For everyone to whom much is given, from him much will be required; and to whom much has been committed, of him, they will ask the more."

Here is a good example of respect. I remember telling my children that I would never embarrass them in from of their friends if they were at our house playing or at their school or in public because I know how important their friends are to them.

But if they did something that I thought was inappropriate or something that I thought wasn't right, when we were alone at home, I would have a discussion with them. I expected better behavior the next time. Unless your child is in danger, you should not be hollering at them or scolding them in public. Please don't do it in front of their peers. It's disrespectful and embarrassing.

There are certain rules that I have at my house, but these rules apply to me as well. One rule was that you don't place your feet on the furniture, and you don't lean back in the chairs because you could break them. So when I would see one of my children sitting on the chair incorrectly, I would always tap them on the shoulder and say, "Sweetie, don't sit in the chair like that. You could break or damage it."

I always addressed my daughters as sweetie or darling, and I never spoke to them in a voice that would be demeaning toward them. I always wanted to show respect and love. How I spoke to them as the first man in their lives was important to me, and it set the tone for them to expect it from all men whom they chose to be around.

So please be careful how you speak to your children. One night, we were all sitting around, watching TV, and I got up to go to the kitchen. I noticed that one of my twin daughters was sitting on the edge of the couch and not on the couch, so I did my normal routine and tapped her on the shoulder. I said gently, "Sweetie, don't sit on the couch like that. You can break it."

Then I proceeded to the kitchen to get a snack. After getting my snack, I noticed that she was still sitting on the edge. She was in the same position as when I first approached her. This was odd because we all knew the rules, and normally, when I asked them to do something, it was usually corrected pretty quickly.

So I followed protocol and went through my ritual by tapping her on the shoulder. I said to her in a gentle voice, "Sweetie, you probably didn't hear Daddy, but I said don't sit on the couch that way because you can break or damage it." She looked up at me with those round eyes. I could only see the white in her eyes because we had dimmed the lights for the movie.

She said to me, "Daddy, I am not sitting on the couch. I am sitting on the arm of the couch!"

OMG! Now listen, I didn't say this was easy. Anyone who has raised a child will tell you that you are going to face challenges. I mean plenty of challenges. That's why the first step we shared was who is influencing you.

I needed God's help. If you were thinking that every nerve in my body was trembling, you would be correct. If you think that I wanted to holler at her, you would be correct. She still was not moving. Okay, let's examine this situation. Technically, she was correct. It is the arm of the couch, but the arm is still a part of the couch. So technically, I was right also.

Let's look closer. Did she know what I was talking about? Absolutely, positively, she did. This is all about children growing up and us being parents. They are going to act one way, and you are going to act another way. But let me just pause and say, "It's more important how you act as a parent than it is how they act as a child." I gathered myself, took a deep breath, and said in a gentle but not as gentle voice, and no sweetie or darling this time came out of my mouth, but still, I used a voice of respect and authority.

I called her by her whole name, "Tara Antoinette Smith, will you please not sit on the arm of the couch that way please." I tell you, the child moved and set on the couch correctly. But what I learned that night would help me raise an amazing darling. I showed her that night that I could respect her point of view and not make a big deal out of it. Although we could have argued about the arm is part of the couch, none of that really mattered. For me, it was an awesome learning experience.

Things to Remember

1. Your words and actions determine the level of respect you receive from your children.
2. Your words have power. They can push your children away from you or bring them close to you.
3. As parents, our words should be encouraging and uplifting.
4. Speaking the right words can change negative behavior.
5. Prayer and God's Word help in producing a positive outcome.
6. Always approach issues with prayer.
7. If you want to know the character of parents, ask their children.
8. Respect is taught. It is not automatic.
9. Train your children by showing them love and kindness.
10. A person who is respectful is careful not to embarrass others.

Reflections

1. I will forgive those who negatively impacted my life with mean and hurtful words. My prayer:

_____

_____

_____

_____

_____

2. How do I feel when I am disrespected?

_____

_____

_____

_____

3. I promise, from this day forward, I will be careful what I say and how I say it!

4. If my words have had a negative impact on my children, I will do the following:

- Say I am sorry and mean it.
- Take responsibility for my actions.
- Practice saying the right words.
- Ask God for help.
- Forgive myself and move forward.
- Handle my children with love and kindness.

STEP 6

TEACH YOUR CHILDREN SELF-RESPECT

If you don't respect yourself, how can you respect others? When do you learn to respect yourself, how do you respect yourself, and who teaches you to respect yourself? All these are great questions, and I can't wait to discuss them with you because most of the time, this step is assumed and not taught.

You and I both know that we can't assume anything, especially when it comes to our children. One of the biggest reasons that our children grow up and don't respect themselves is because they don't feel respected by their parents in a lot of cases. They have low self-esteem because of the way they have been treated. Our choice of words plays a huge part in how our children perceive us. When you can calmly discuss matters of importance with your children, they will pick up on how they should respond to you and others.

It is not helpful or necessary to holler or use profane language when your child does something to upset you. Nor does it help to say, "I am the adult. I pay the bills in this house." They know that all too well. That is not the issue that upset you! Stick with the issue at hand and calm down before you cause a wound in your child's spirit that can affect them for a long time. I am sure if your child is a preteen or teenager, he or she has heard the story of who the boss is in his or her home too many times.

Many times we look at things wrongly. Our children are not attacking our adulthood. Remember, they are a gift from God, but when he blessed us with them, he gave us an assignment with instructions on how he wants us to raise them. When you have a child, that assignment is yours for you to complete. If your children grow up respecting themselves, it's because you taught them to do so. If they grow up not respecting themselves, it's because you failed to teach them too.

Proverbs 22:6 (NKJV) tells us how to help our children. "Train up a child in the way he should go, and when he is old, he will not depart from it." If you train them in the right way, they will hold to those principles.

You can take the time to train them or decide not to train them. Either way, when they grow older, they will still be your children and reflect your training or your lack of training. But can I tell you who you are hurting when you don't train them in the way they should go? You are hurting them and yourself. They have a life to live, and when you don't take time to teach them, you are not valuing them like you should, and they will not value themselves like they should.

Many times children will grow up not learning to value or respect themselves. I know that all children learn differently, but most learn by how they are treated. They go on to treat others the way they were treated. And if they are not able to love and respect themselves, they will be easily manipulated by others who are less important than you and who will never love them like you do.

Therefore, at all costs as parents, we must avoid using belittling tactics when dealing with our children, as it pertains to correction or other things that come up that may be difficult or sensitive to discuss with them. We are responsible for building their self-esteem so they can learn how to respect themselves and others. Here are some things that your child will never forget and will appreciate you for doing them:

Number 1, if you are entering your child's room, knock first and ask for permission to enter. By doing this, you are showing them that you respect their privacy. They will know that you care about their personal space and realize they are valued in your eyesight. How can they not value themselves when you have so much respect for them? You are not just telling your children, but you are demonstrating it by respecting their space.

This may seem like a small gesture, but it is huge. Your child will learn that they should never walk into a room without knocking first. They will never allow anyone to walk in their space without knocking or expecting them to knock. You are not doing this for you. You are doing it for your child. You are saying, "I respect you even though you are a child." You are teaching with your actions.

Number 2, you want your children to think for themselves. Make it a habit to ask your children what they think about different things as you engage them in conversation. It is good that they can voice how they feel about things in a nonjudgmental atmosphere. Their opinions are included and important to family discussions. You want them to develop their ability to think and give their opinions. A child without an opinion will always follow the opinions and suggestions of others.

I fought hard for this one. I did not want my children to be followers of other people's ideas only. They needed strong minds of their own. I desired and wanted their leadership skills to be way above average. They needed to think for themselves.

I remember when my oldest daughter got to the age where she could go places with her friends. On this particular day, one of her friends stopped by unannounced and wanted to go to the movie and asked my daughter if she wanted to go with her. My daughter got excited and ran to where I was and asked me, "Daddy, can I go to the movie with Kwanza?" I could see the excitement in her eyes and hear the enthusiasm in her voice. Now I knew most of my daughter's friends.

Parents, it is important to know your children's friends. I put emphasis on it because it is vitally important that you do. I knew Kwanza and her family well, so I wasn't about to disappoint my daughter and tell her no. Kwanza was a great kid and a leader as well. So I said to my daughter, "Sure, Tan, you can go to the movie, but let me asked you a question, 'Are you going to the movie because you want to go, or are you going because Kwanza asked you too?'"

I am not naive. I knew the answer to that question before asking it. Her answer was, "It's because I want to go." I gave her money and told her to have fun. But I took that opportunity to get her to think about what she wanted to do in the future and not what someone else wanted her to do. If you want your child to respect and value their time, you have to teach them. Otherwise, they will value what others are doing and respect it more than they value what they are doing and their decisions.

How your child views him or herself is how they will treat themselves and allow others to treat them as well. When you tell your child they can't go someplace, explain why they can't go. Don't just say you can't go, because I said so! If it's something you don't want them to do, give them an explanation as to why they can't do it. When you don't want them to wear certain clothes, meet with them in their room and have a conversation about it.

There was a rule in our house that whatever they were dealing with, we would come together and figure out a solution. This rule kept us talking a lot because it was always something that we had to deal with and come up with a solution. I remember my oldest getting some clothing for Christmas from one of her aunts. It was a blue jean miniskirt. When she opened the box and I saw it, I thought, *O'Lawd! Why is someone giving this to my child?* I thought, *We will have to figure this out sooner or later*. Well, the time came sooner than later.

It was a nice calm evening, and we had finished dinner. Our daughter was getting her clothes out for the next day. This was strange because she would normally wait until the same morning to get her clothes ready for that day. I know it's not ideal to wait until the same day to get your clothes for that day, but hey, she had managed to do it successfully for so long, why try to stop her now?

However, this time, something was different! It was the big day. The weather had been nice all week, and it was time for the big blue miniskirt. It was worthy of the night before school preparation. If you think your child doesn't know you, think again, because they do. She made an announcement to me that she was wearing her blue jean dress to school tomorrow. Did you notice she didn't call it a miniskirt?

But trust me, it was a miniskirt. Children are very smart. They know how you think. So I had to be smart too. I didn't fuss, I said, "Really?"

"Yes," she said. "I have been waiting a month, and now that the weather is nice, I am wearing it tomorrow."

I said, "Tan, you know this is too short to wear to school, and it's not who you are."

She replied, "But, Dad, my auntie gave this to me for a Christmas present. What am I supposed to do with it?"

During a time like this, if you are not careful, someone else can run your household. It doesn't have to be a relative. It can be a friend or a stranger. I can't tell you how many children are being influenced by someone other than their parents? Most television shows have more power than the parents. For the most part, this is because the child has grown up without any identity. They haven't been appreciated for who they are. And now they don't value who they are. So now they are influenced by whoever they think they respect.

Why? Because they are not feeling respected by the most important people in their lives. How unfortunate it is for a child to look for love and acceptance in all the wrong places. What a negative effect on their self-esteem. This is where preset rules can be very helpful. I am not talking about rules that work for the parents but are not good for the children.

Remember, I shared with you that we have a rule in our house where we could talk about any problem and come up with a solution. Thank God because we used that rule a lot. I said to Tan, "Just because someone gives you something, doesn't mean you have to wear it. They shouldn't decide who you are and what you wear. You are the one who chooses how you want to be represented. When you are getting ready for school, you decide what is appropriate and how you should look, not everyone else, and I am here to tell you, this blue jean miniskirt is not appropriate for you to wear."

So at that point, she started to whine and get teary eyed. So I said, "Let's talk about it. You really like the miniskirt that your aunt gave you?"

"Yes," she said.

"So what can we do to make it more like Tan because this doesn't remind me of you and your character?" She had no suggestions, so I said, "What if you wore some black tights with the skirt. Would that work for you?"

"Then I can wear it?" she asked, all bright-eyed.

"Yes, that works for me," I said.

But it didn't really work for me; however, sometimes as parents, we meet them more than halfway. Now before this incident, my daughter had always been a conservative-dressing young lady, and we have never had an issue with the way she dressed before.

Now after that episode, I noticed my child never wore the dress again. Months passed, and I realized the blue jean miniskirt was not in her weekly rotation, not even in her monthly rotation. Don't get me wrong, I didn't necessarily want it to be in her rotation, but I was curious as to why it wasn't, so I asked. What she experienced the day she wore the short miniskirt to school helped her to realize that she didn't need clothes to identify her, and she was the identifier of the clothes she wanted to wear.

Most any other kid would have heard the words of how cute the dress looked from their peers—but not my child. You see, she had established herself as being self-confident in her own skin, and she didn't have to have the latest fashion or other people to identify who she was. She did not seek her friend's approval or their admiration concerning her style; however, it was different this time around.

Since they admired her, they teased her for what she wore that day. They made comments like, "Tan, what do you have on?" "Tan, did your dad see you before you came to school today?" "Tan, I can't believe you wore that to school?"

You see, her peers could wear something like that, but they had higher standards for Tan because of the way she carried herself among her peers.

Now it's one thing to be self-confident, but when your peers respect you and you have confidence in yourself, it's a form of validation. Peers play an important part in your child's life. Their words were more powerful than anything I could have said.

Now let me explain to you that I am not knocking miniskirts. I am just saying it was not how I envisioned my daughter dressing. I have that right to have a vision for them. I am using this as an example of why parents should start early teaching their children self-respect. If it is taught, you can look forward to it being caught by them and demonstrate on the way they live their lives, and others will respect them for who they are and who they represent.

Things to Remember

1. Respect has to be taught. It can't be assumed.
2. When correcting your children, work out the problem with love and understanding.
3. When your children grow up, they will reflect on your training or lack of training.
4. Children need good examples to learn self-respect.
5. Teach your child that their personal space is private.
6. Engage your children in conversation—their opinions matter.
7. Do your best to teach your children good leadership skills.
8. With the best of your ability, make sure your child gets the best teaching and training.
9. Let your children know that you trust them.
10. Teach them to value their time and that of others.

Reflections

Self-respect—knowing that you are valued and deserve to be treated with respect and dignity.

1. Ways to build self-respect in children.

   - Remind them that they are your gift from God, and you love them unconditionally.
   - Be understanding.
   - Always look for the good in them.
   - Encourage them when they don't do well.
   - Tell them that wrong behavior does not make them bad.
   - Listen when your child talks.
   - Never make fun or belittle them.
   - Respect their property and privacy.

Self-esteem—when a child feels good about himself.

2. Ways to build a child's self-esteem.

- Help them make a list of things they do well.
- Allow them to do things on their own.
- Let them help you with a project.
- Take their feeling seriously.
- Teach them that failing is a way to learn how to do things better.
- Praise them for their efforts.
- Don't compare them with others.

INSPIRE YOUR CHILDREN TO SUCCEED

We have discussed that you are the bridge that connects your children to God. You have an awesome assignment to teach your children how to live life to their fullest potential. This includes them striving for excellence in all they do to the best of their ability. This responsibility on the parent to help them succeed is a great one.

Your children are not just living with you. You are a living example for them—which means, what you say and do is being watched and mentally recorded by your children. They will play it back and act it out throughout their lives. What you do places an indelible print on their personalities because that's what they have seen and heard during the crucial times in their lives.

When I say that raising children is a twenty-five-hours-a-day and eight-days-a-week job, I simply mean that you never stop thinking and planning how you can best reach and teach your children in order to help them succeed early in their lives. Parental participation is necessary early in their lives. Eating with them, playing with them, shopping with them, studying with them, encouraging them, going to the park with them, and so many more activities, I could go on and on, but you get the point.

You have to spend time with them. Notice that I didn't say quality time. One of the most deceptive lies ever told was that you just need to spend quality time with your child. Your child doesn't know the difference between quantity versus quality time. They spell love as *time*. You need to spend as much time with them as possible.

In order to raise amazing children, you have to know them and that comes with being involved in their everyday activities. Yes, it is a sacrifice but a worthy one. How can you know them if you are not spending any or very little time with them? How are they going to know which way to go? Joshua 3:9 (NKJV) says, "So Joshua said to the children of Israel, 'Come here, and hear the words of the Lord your God.'"

So you are saying to the children in your family as you train them "to come here and hear the words of their God." You represent God to them, and when they see the Word in action, they will duplicate it because it's all they know.

My wife and I were at the park with our children, and at the pavilion next to ours, there was a family who was using choice words that we didn't use in our family. There are times like that when you can't keep your children from hearing wrong words, but you certainly can make a decision not to use them in your household.

Well, after hearing these words, our baby daughter Amber came to me and said, "Daddy, they are using bad words."

I responded, "I hear them, sweetie."

She kept looking at me because I wasn't moving in their direction to stop them from using such awful language! She was a little confused because this is not how people were to talk, especially younger folks. And for me to just allow this to go on was insane and hypocritical in her mind.

After all, we didn't even use the words "shut up" in our home. If someone did, you could bet that one of my children would tell on the one who did. We used words like "be quiet" or "hush!" I know you are thinking, *Seriously? Your children couldn't use the word shut up?* Hey, these were my rules in my house, and I set the example. I couldn't say shut up either.

My rules were for the family, not something to dictate to my children. If I said something that was out of line, they checked me on it. They let me know that we didn't use those kinds of words in our house. You would have thought they were the parents, and they took pleasure in letting me know I was in the wrong.

When we made it home, I explained to Amber that Daddy couldn't tell other children what to do or say. Our rules only applied to our house. Other parent rules could be different for their home. Then I reiterated to her that we don't ever talk like that.

But that's how we teach our children to succeed early in life. We set high standards in our homes and allow that to be their guide to a successful life. Remember, you are the bridge to direct your child to God. Both parent and child will make many mistakes on the road leading to success, but when we stay focused and maintain the course with Christ as our leader, we will achieve our goals. Setbacks are temporary, but comebacks are mandatory.

Don't be afraid to make mistakes in life big or small, and don't be ashamed to own up to your mistakes to your children. When you can own the errors that you make to your child and be willing to address your faults with them, you are showing them how to address issues in life. And it's never too early for you to start. It can be vital to their success going forward in life.

I can remember when I had to discipline my daughter Chara for something that she had done, or I thought she had done. I have twins, and I disciplined the wrong one. But when I found out, it was too late. Her twin sister had gotten off totally free of punishment, and I had punished an innocent child.

Man, did I feel bad. I had to do something right away to make things right. So I immediately, upon realizing my mistake, went straight to her room and sincerely apologized with tears in my eyes. I told her that I was sorry and asked her to forgive me.

She said, "Daddy, that's okay. I forgive you!" She gave me a big hug and asked if I was going to punish Tara, her twin.

That was one of the greatest lessons that I learned from my child about parenting. And yes, I have had many moments where I learned how to be a better parent by communicating with my children. But this one served me greatly, and I am still benefiting from that moment.

You see, after a week had passed and everything had settled down and the incident had slipped my mind, Chara stopped me in the hallway and asked me if I was still sorry. It had been a week since this all happened, and I wasn't thinking about it. So I asked her, "Sorry about what, sweetie?"

She said, "You know."

I answered, "I don't remember, darling. Tell me."

She said, "You remember when you punished me by mistake and you said you were sorry?"

I said, "Oh yes. Daddy is still sorry and feels so bad about what happened." Then I asked her if she still forgives me for what I did. She said yes and gave me a big hug.

You see, this wasn't the first time that I had made a mistake. Trust me, I have made many. But I couldn't remember saying that I was sorry for something to Chara before. It was, for sure, the first time that she recognized that I had made a mistake. I could see how this brought me down a little closer to her level. A lot of times, our children tend to think that we are perfect and without fault. Now all of a sudden, she saw me not as this perfect being who had been placed on this earth to always correct and discipline them. I tell you, this really changed my life when it came to raising my children.

I started looking for reasons to apologize. I didn't want to be seen as flawless in their eyes, and the more I could apologize, the more they could see the human errors that we all make and the more I could explain that our God and Savior Jesus is the only one who is without faults—knowing that they would find out my faults anyway. It was good to be transparent early and often in their lives. It gave me the opportunity to introduce to them the scripture that read, "For all have sinned and fall short of the glory of God" (Romans 3:23, NKJV).

We do not want our children to think that they can't make blunders. Life doesn't exist without them. You cannot succeed in life unless you realize that you are going to have some mishaps, and the sooner you learn this fact, the better off our children are prepared for the life that they are going to face. I can't express enough how important it is for you to be on your children's level and become their biggest cheerleader.

It doesn't mean that you are their friend and not their parents. What it means is that you are taking the time to relate and understand them. You are willing to listen to the little things that matter most to them. It also means you are not too busy to spend time with the gifts God has blessed you with, and you are willing to do whatever it takes for them to have success in life.

Again, in the beginning, you are speaking the Word of God into their lives and showing them which way to go. You are letting your child know that you will always be there for them. Later, after you have decreased in their life, you have witnessed Christ increase in their life. That lets you know that you have been the bridge you needed to be for them. You raised them with integrity and the knowledge of God. Your prayers and faith in God's Word will be demonstrated as they draw closer and closer to Christ and live as productive Christians. Remember, "things just don't happen. Somebody has to make them happen."

Before a building contractor builds a house, he will first build the foundation. Without a foundation, the house wouldn't be able to stand and endure the rain and storms that are sure to come. Likewise, because you have accepted God as your Savior, you have equipped your children with a solid foundation on which they can stand against the wrong that surrounds them in this world, and they will make a tremendous difference for themselves, their families, and for all who know them. This is all possible because we first sought the kingdom of God for our children, and they are in God's hand. There is nothing that was created on earth without God.

To attempt to live a life without God is crazy, and to try to raise children without God guiding us is ludicrous. God is the beginning and the end, the alpha and the omega. Everything starts with him and ends with him. And to raise amazing children, you want to start with him, stay with him, and finish with him. Then you will raise amazing children.

Jeremiah 2:9 (NKJV) says, "All your children shall be taught by the Lord, and great shall be the peace of your children."

Things to Remember

1. Your children should learn how to succeed through your guidance.
2. What you say and do is being mentally recorded by your children.
3. Parental participation is necessary early in your children's lives.
4. You represent God to your children. They will try to duplicate what you say and do.
5. Be very selective in the language you use in teaching your child to do well.
6. Children need to know that parents can and will make a mistake, but God is perfect.
7. A wise parent will apologize when wrong.
8. Communicating is necessary for being a great parent.
9. You have the power to change your child's life for their eternal good.
10. Parents have a unique responsibility for their children's well-being.

MORE REFLECTIONS FROM MY HEART

CONCLUSION

I taught my children to be overcomers because there will always be challenges in life. My daughter Chara was faced with a tough challenge. Even though she was a twin, her personality was different from that of her sister. Everybody from kindergarten through high school had expectations of Chara on the basis of her sister's behavior and performances.

Even if a child is not a twin but has another sibling who went to the same school before he or she did, they face the challenge of being judged by what their sister or brother did. Teachers will often associate and make comparisons because they expect them to be like their siblings.

However, it can be even worse when you are a twin. If Chara had a teacher that her sister had for a class, she started to make announcements to the teachers on the first day of class that she was not Tara. She didn't want to be compared with her sister. Imagine the internal struggles a child faces year after year, when judged by the failure or success of a sibling.

Chara entered a beauty pageant, and during the interview process, she had to explain why she wanted to be Miss CDC. She was having a hard time expressing her thoughts on paper as to why she wanted to be Miss CDC at her school. So around eight o'clock that night, I said to her, "Chara, just write down why you want to be in the pageant in the first place, and that should do."

She said, "To be honest with you, Dad, I want to do something that Tara has not done. Everyone has always compared us! She has the most outgoing personality, she is popular, and she makes better grades than I do. And, Dad, she doesn't even study as hard as I do. So I just want to do something she hasn't done so I can say, this is what Chara has done."

Now, as her father, I could see the real problem, and we had to deal with it head-on.

So I said, "Chara, first, I want to apologize to you." She asked why, and I said, "Because you took after your dad when it comes to book smarts, and Tara took after her mother for her book smarts. Tara doesn't have to study as hard as you do to learn." Ironically, Chara is named after me, Charles, and Tara carries her mother's middle name. Although that has nothing to do with their ability to learn. My wife is as smart as they come. As for me, I had to work as hard as possible to make passing grades.

I explained to Chara that her mother and Tara could read a book one time and remember the content of the book and pass a test. We might have to read the same book three times to get what they got out of the book the first time they read it. But it's not important how many times you have to read the book to remember the material to pass a test. The important thing is that you get and understand the material that you are looking for.

I told her it was her responsibility to get what she needed to succeed, regardless of how hard she had to work. You can accomplish anything if you are willing to work for it. It was one o'clock in the morning before we went to bed, but it was well worth the time for my child. She went on to place second in the pageant contest, but more importantly, she graduated from Tougaloo College with honors. She is an overcomer.

I taught my children not to place limits on themselves. My baby Amber wanted to be in the IB program (International Baccalaureate). She had been looking forward to it for a whole year. But when the time came, she had changed her mind. I asked her why. She said that she was talking to some friends that were in the program last year, and it was too hard, so they dropped out.

I said, "What does that have to do with you?"

She explained, "I don't want to get to class and find out that it's too hard and have to drop out."

I explained to her that we don't make decisions about our lives based on what other students experience. We tackled problems head-on. One of my favorite quotes is "Tough times never last, but tough people do" by Dr. Robert Schuller. I told Amber that there were no students at that school as tough as she was. I explained to her that she had great study habits and was more disciplined than any other student.

She said, "Daddy, it's too late now because the deadline has passed for interviews."

I told her, "It's never too late to get what you want out of life! If you want it, just go for it."

I contacted the school the next day, which was Friday. That Saturday morning, I was sitting in the lobby waiting on my daughter while she was being interviewed for the IB program. On Wednesday of the next week, we were jumping up and down, celebrating her entry into the IB program.

She went on to excel in the program and had the best time of her life. I did too because I was one of the parents who got a chance to travel to Jamaica with her on their trip! We had a great time. We have to show our children that they can make happen what they want to happen. Just don't be afraid. God has them, and they are going to be okay.

I have learned that if nobody else encourages your child. You better be there encouraging them every step of the way! There are people who could be careless about how your child feels. You have to keep your child lifted up in prayer and encourage them in all their endeavors.

My oldest daughter had a substitute teacher in one of her classes. This substitute teacher was going to be at the school for the whole year because the regular teacher was on maternity leave. My daughter was taking a test, and she completed it fairly quickly. She turned her paper in, and her substitute teacher looked at it and made the comment, "If the rest of you are solving the problem like she did on her paper, you are doing it incorrectly."

She instructed them to do it the other way. My daughter said to the teacher, "Oh! I see now. Can I have my paper back?"

In front of the whole class, she told my daughter, "No, you can't have your paper back."

Now she had just helped the entire class by using my girl's paper.

She came home in tears, explaining to me what happened and that she was not going to try to pass that class because of the way the teacher treated her.

So I said to her, "Are you going to allow someone else the power to determine your future and not try anymore?"

She said, "But, Dad, that wasn't fair!"

I said, "But, Tan, she is a substitute teacher, and she is learning. She may be a great teacher one day."

My daughter interrupted me and said, "No, Daddy! She will never be a good teacher. I don't know why they have her there."

I explained to her that now she has an advantage because she knows how she operates now, and she doesn't have to turn her paper in first anymore. You can't allow the thinking or behavior of someone else to influence your decision to be your very best. Always be the very best that you can be regardless of the setbacks that you face. You will always come back stronger than ever before.

Now let's be honest. I didn't like the way the teacher handled that situation at all. But I have never bad-mouthed a teacher in front of my children, and I wasn't going to start then. For me to behave negatively toward the teacher was not going to help my daughter. My child needed to know I believed in her, and I needed her to bounce back stronger than ever before.

These things will happen in life, and you have to be ready to deal with them. But believe me, I dealt with the teacher one-on-one, and she assured me that the papers were graded on a curve, and my daughter's grades were not affected. With our God on our side and in our life, we can always handle what's wrong in the right way. Tanya passed the class with an A average and never looked back.

I have always wanted my girls to be leaders and not followers. Every child is different, and you have to embrace their uniqueness. Just because a child is different than their siblings and maybe more challenging does not necessarily mean that's a bad thing. As parents, it should never be voiced that we wish they were like their siblings, who may have been less challenging.

Our job is to go to God and ask him to help us to be better-equipped parents to raise our more challenging children with whom God has blessed us. As you have read the examples that I shared to get my point across on the 7 steps to raising amazing children, you would guess that Tara would have been my most challenging child to raise.

She liked to claim that she made things easier for her baby sister Amber. She challenged rules and a lot of times questioned our motives as to why we even had rules. I don't know about making it better for Amber because, as parents, we embraced Amber's uniqueness just like we appreciated her uniqueness.

I have never admitted to Tara or anybody else that she was my most-challenging child. But what I will say is that I could have used Tara as an example throughout this book because we had so many experiences. And I have had to ask God so many times, "Lord, show me how to lead, direct, and manage your child," and he has never failed me. If I didn't know God, my daughters would not be where they are today, and I wouldn't be where I am as a parent.

I want all of you to know that there is nothing too hard for God. My baby Tara showed us a message that she received on Facebook the other day, which one of her friends sent her. She was thanking her for inviting her to church so many years ago. The friend didn't remember the name of the church, but she remembered getting saved, and she wanted to thank Tara for that. Tara invited many friends to church, as did my other children, and I would go and pick them up. Challenging? Are you kidding me? We need to embrace our gifts from God and train them up to be soldiers for him.

Whatever we teach our children, they pass it on to their children, and it gets passed on to the generations following. If you are raising one child or several children, that means God has chosen you to be your best as a parent. It means that you have the assignment to love, teach, and care for the most precious love gifts from heaven. May these seven steps help you as you raise your children to be amazing!

MY TAKEAWAY FROM THESE SEVEN STEPS

- _____
- _____
- _____
- _____
- _____
- _____
- _____

Lord, with your help, I will live by the principles I learned from the *7 Steps to Raising Amazing Children* and always do my best to keep myself in right standing with you and your word. I am an amazing parent, raising amazing children.

MY FATHER'S INFLUENCE IN MY LIFE

Letter from Tara Baker

The biggest influences of my dad can be seen in my marriage and in the way I raise my kids. But when I really think about it, my whole being and who I am is because of you. So basically, you have influenced my whole life.

As I grew up, you weren't my favorite parent. That's probably no secret because let's be honest, I was your most challenging child. I like to think I made you the great parent you are today. I didn't always obey the rules, and sometimes, I was sarcastic in my obedience.

For example, remember Disney World? You told me to get off the rail and stand up. Well, I stood up and sat right back down on the rail. To me, sitting wasn't hurting anybody, and you said to stand up, not remain standing. But now that I am grown, I can think of reasons why sitting on the rail was dangerous. But how you handled it as a parent influenced my parenting today.

Raising Kids How You Raised Us

You promised you would never embarrass us or discipline us in front of our peers. That taught me that as a parent, I must have patience. So daily, I think, "Now how would my dad handle this?"

You celebrated us weekly. We had "Doughnut Day" with Dad. No specific reason, just time spent with Dad. Of course, I had to keep that going. Braxton is only two and doesn't really understand that it's once a week we eat donuts (because he asks every day), but on the actual day, he is elated.

You listened to us. I got in trouble a lot. And when I was in trouble, you compared my behavior to my oldest sister, Zatanya—usually stating what she wouldn't do. This made me jealous, and I expressed my disdain of the comparison. From that day on, you promised never to compare us again. I still got punished, but you kept your promise, and I was never compared again.

So now I know I can learn from my kids. I welcome the day they express their concerns and pray that I can answer them with the fairness you showed us.

Marriage

Well, I wanted a husband that could be a father to my kids like you were to us—also a man who loved the Lord, didn't use profanity, didn't drink or smoke, and wanted to be an active father and patient with a super extra wife! Surely, another man like that didn't exist, right? Lucky me, I saw those dad-like qualities immediately in my husband, and I quickly said, "I do," to him. Here we stand eleven years later.

You've influenced the way I eat, the way I communicate, the way I think positively, and my Christian walk. I'm grateful for you, Dad. I'm proud of you too. I can't wait for you to publish your book. The world needs more fathers like you.

Letter from Chara McGill

In 2008, I walked into my premarital therapy session with a smile on my face alongside my fiancé, now husband. "We're getting married, and I can't wait!" I announced. My therapist didn't look too excited for me because this particular session was scheduled to pull up any childhood trauma from the past, particularly stemming from our parents. Apparently, she'd seen couples unable to make it pass such segments. She prepared herself for the worst.

My therapist began the session. "Chara, please write out all your disappointments you've experienced during your childhood from your father, and your fiancé will do the same." I sat for a minute, and my therapist looked up at me, assuming that something was wrong.

"It's okay," she said. "There is nothing to be ashamed of. You can start writing now."

I looked back at her in confusion.

"Oh no, I'm finished," I stated.

"But, Chara, you didn't write anything down. I need you to take this assignment seriously," she exclaimed.

"I am! I'm finished."

It was as if my therapist was upset that my paper was blank, so I felt the need to explain. "My paper is blank because my father *never* disappointed me, whether in childhood or adulthood. I have no disappointments!" I thought that my therapist would move on to the next question, but she proceeded to tell me, "That's impossible." She expressed that there must be something that my father did to cause some disappointment in my life, something that he must have done! She wouldn't let it go.

Finally, because she would not let up, I said, "Well, yea…there was this one time." The therapist sat forward, listening intensely. "My father wouldn't let my sister and I ride the bus to school because he wanted to take us personally. I was looking forward to riding the bus to be like the cool kids, but my father—he wanted to take us to eat doughnuts before school." The therapist sat back. Needless to say, my fiancé chuckled.

I have the esteemed honor to write this letter to tell all who may read this book that my father, Mr. Charles Smith, has never, in my thirty-nine years of living, disappointed me. It's something about the way he raised my sisters and me that has caused us to all live life to not disappoint him. As for me, when I was in elementary school, when I was tempted to steal, to cheat, or even curse to be like the popular kids, I thought of my father and changed my behavior to align with the rules.

When I was in high school, I was tempted to skip school, sneak out of class, or act a fool in some way. I thought of my father and again, changed my behavior to align with what's right. In college, when I was tempted to "go wild," explore college behaviors, drink, party—you name it—the same thing happened. I thought of my father and simply decided to steer right. Why, because I didn't want to disappoint my father, the man who never disappointed me.

As a child and as an adult, my father didn't just teach me to be my best. He lived his best in front of me. His methods, his words of wisdom, advice, and even correction didn't go into one ear and out the next because what he said, he also lived. He's a man of great character that I admire. His work ethic taught me to never give up.

His character goes before his name. His love for his family wasn't just shown behind closed doors. He lived his life to please his heavenly Father, and in return, it made me want to live the exact same way. Before I knew God for myself, I made my decisions in life through the lens of "Will my dad [Charles] approve?"

When I turned twenty-four and built an authentic personal relationship with Christ, that's when I realized that my dad and I's relationship was the bridge to help me live for Christ's approval. Parents are supposed to set an example of how to live and navigate through this world. The example my father has set makes me feel like I can conquer this world.

In the words of Mary (when Jesus was getting ready to turn water into wine), she looked at the servant as said to him, "Whatever

He tells you, do it" (John 2:5). I say the same to you, the reader. Whatever my father has instructed you to do in this book, do it.

> May your children one day declare that you've never disappointed them!
>
> —Chara McGill,
> author of *Chara's Story:*
> *Trying to Get to a Place Called Pretty.*
> *How I Discovered the Truth About Beauty*

Letter from Zatanya Collins

Oh, where do I even start? My whole life has been an exercise of continued life lessons that I live by today. My dad is an amazing human being who has been extolling wisdom to me my entire life. To this day, when I need counsel, it is my dad who I turn to.

Let me first say, the best way to influence anyone is to model the behavior you want to instill. My dad lives that life. There was no, do what I say, not what I do. It is do what I do. He is a strong Christian who is very active in the church. What's even more remarkable is what you see at church is exactly how he lives his life everywhere—at home and at work. He is the most genuine person I know.

My dad is a strong believer in accountability, and he does not believe in making excuses. I remember in my early years, even though I lived within walking distance from school, my dad would wake me up, take me to breakfast, and drop me off.

I didn't really appreciate how good I had it, and he would often have to tell me several times to get up and get dressed. After struggling with this for several weeks, my dad finally put his foot down. He told me, "I am not waking you up tomorrow. If you aren't ready on time, you will get left." So the next day, I didn't wake up on time, and I got left. I could not believe he left me!

From that day on, it was my responsibility to be ready on time. If I did, I got a ride to school, and if I didn't, I had to walk, and on top of that, if I was late for school, there were consequences.

Often as parents, it's easy to get in the habit of doing everything for our kids, making sure they get up and get dressed and having to fuss with them on a daily basis about the exact same thing. Sometimes, the best way to learn a lesson is to let them fail and experience the consequences of that failure.

That was the lesson I learned that day. I am not going to say I was on time from that day forward, but I will say the responsibility of being on time was no longer my parents, but on me. Life lesson from Dad, kids will never learn responsibly if they aren't given responsibility.

My dad was very active in our lives growing up. He was the PTA president, the band booster club president, and he chaperoned every school trip. Everyone knew my dad, even my college friends! However, his presence was never overbearing or controlling.

My dad did not believe in embarrassing his kids. He understood the fragility of teenage self-esteem. As a result, I was never afraid of my dad being around all the time. I knew he would never embarrass me. By watching the way my dad lived his life, how he lives by the faith that he proclaims, how he is constantly present, and how he treats people on a daily basis has been the biggest influence in my life.

Letter from Amber Palmer

"Follow me as I follow Christ, and one day, you'll follow Christ, and others will follow you." I may have been in lower elementary school when I first heard my dad say that, and at the time, I didn't really understand it. I was going to follow my dad for the rest of my life because he was perfect in my eyes! My dad was enough, and if I followed him, I was surely going to be a great person.

When I was in high school, I attended a youth retreat with my church, and while on the retreat, we were asked to enjoy nature, talk to God, and allow him to talk to you. While I appreciate God's creation, I'm not a fan of being outside. This particular day, I enjoyed watching the grass sway, sitting under a tree, and gazing at the lake.

A weird question randomly came to mind. As much as I wanted to not think about that question, I could not stop thinking about it, and I began to sob. I cannot imagine waking up on the weekends and not seeing my dad on his knees in the living room, praying or sitting at the table reading his Bible.

I remember losing a very expensive camera one day at Disney World, and I was distraught, but when I told my dad that I lost it, he simply said, "Okay!" Who could be so forgiving? What would I do without my dad? After a few minutes of sobbing, I "snapped back" to reality and reminded myself that all is well. My day was just fine.

As I continued to sit and think, a peace of God came upon me, and that quote came to mind. "Follow me as I follow Christ, and one day, you'll follow Christ, and others will follow you." That was it. It was my time to stop worshipping my dad and worship Christ for myself.

So how has my dad influenced my life? He led me to Christ. He didn't just take me to church, read scriptures to me, tell me Bible stories, or teach me how to pray. He did all those things (and more), but most importantly, he showed me that professing that you love God means nothing if your actions do not show it.

He was (and is) a living example of what it means to follow Christ. Yes, we all make mistakes, and yes, we all have flaws, but Dad taught me that Jesus didn't come to earth for the perfect. He came for the flawed, the sinners, and the ones who need him the most. He came for us.

I have two phenomenal sons, and one daughter and I hope my husband and I are able to create wonderful memories like my dad did with me, such as "Doughnut Tuesday." We had the best bakery doughnuts every Tuesday, family trips, car rides to school (I never rode the bus to school) while listening to inspirational messages (from Dr. Tony Evans, Zig Ziegler, and/or Charles Stanley), and special birthday dinners. While those memories are great, the greatest impact I hope to have on my children is to be an example of what it means to follow Christ, just as my dad did for me.

SPECIAL THANKS

I want to say a special thanks to my bishop, pastor, and mentor, Ronnie C. Crudup, the founder of New Horizon Church International in Jackson, Mississippi. Thank you, Bishop, for seeing the gift God blessed me with to work with children. I had no idea that God had placed me here on earth to work with children.

Because of you and the faith and trust you placed in me, I have no doubt that I am sewing in my calling for which God placed me on earth to do. Thank you for allowing God to use you to be a blessing to my family and me, as well as many other families that have succeeded under your leadership at New Horizon Church International. Bishop, because of the programs and the many activities that you put in place, you have helped us raise our children. Thank you for creating that village that is so needed.

To my guardian angel, Author Susan Hairston, the editor for this book. Words cannot express my gratitude and the appreciation that I have for you. God truly blessed me when I met you and your husband, who prayed for this book before it was in your hands. Thank you all so much for caring for me.

To Pastor Tonya Ware, who got me started writing in a book writing class that she held. She is an author and singer herself and nominated for a Stellar Award for her worship album *Signature of God!* Thank you for taking time out of your busy schedule to help me, along with others, to tell our stories.

To my church family who has supported me all these years. I thank you for bringing your children out to the events and believing in my wife and me and allowing us to care for your precious children.

To my siblings, Jessie, Jim, Clayborn, Clay Jr., and my baby sister Mary. I want to thank you guys for always believing and trusting in me.

To my church children, who grew up through the children's ministry and are now grown with children of their own. Thank you for passing the scriptures and songs on to your children. Thank you for encouraging me. This book is for you.

To Lauren Nicole Sinclair, our church daughter, who worked for me for a year in my business but impacted me with quality and professionalism for a lifetime. You are now using that same quality and professionalism in your business *Laurenicole Designs*. You always asked me, "When are you going to write a book?" Thank you, Nicole.

To Dr. Kameron Harris, who grew up in my home with my girls and was just like one of my own. Thank you for always supporting our work for the children and being there for me every time I needed you. You and your family will always be special to us.

To my girls, Zatanya, Chara, Tara, and Amber, one powerful way that God shows his love for me each and every day is through you ladies. What an awesome way to show love. I am better than blessed. I love you so much! Thanks for being who you are.

When I say I am blessed, I really am. With four daughters that I adore, I am grateful for my four sons-in-law that I love and admire. They are a blessing! To Drew, John, Ali, and Nick, thanks for being the kind of spouses that I would have handpicked for my daughters if they hadn't beat me to it! Gail and I love and appreciate how you love and treat our daughters and grandchildren.

To the honey of my life, my beautiful wife Gail, marrying you was an upgrade for me, and I have God to thank for that. But I want to thank you for sticking to God's plan by staying by my side because surely, he created you for me. I love you, Mrs. Smith, and I always will.

IN MEMORY OF MY MOTHER

Finally, to Cora Lee, my mom! I wish you were here in the flesh to see how you raised me. I feel your spirit present with me every day. Your godly principles have been passed on to your grandchildren and now your great-grandchildren. I know you are smiling and happy about that.

You would always tell me during your latter years that I needed my own personal relationship with Jesus Christ. I know now that you knew that I was holding on to you too tight and too long. I had no idea what you were saying because you were everything to me, and I felt that you were all I needed. When God called you home, although it was hard, I finally realized what you meant because only Jesus could fill the void I had. I want you to know that I have tried to be that bridge for my children like you were for me. Thank you, Momma. You are the best! I love you, and I always will!

ABOUT THE AUTHOR

When we go through something, ideally, we should grow through what we go through. This way, we will learn from our past. I remember the things that I went through as a child, and I would always say that, I like or I don't like the way that turned out, and I made sure to avoid doing that again. If we all remember our past as children and the things we liked or didn't like and what was good for us and what wasn't, we would be more careful with the steps that we take to raise our own children. We all want to raise amazing children.